EXCESSIVE SODIUM
a collection of poems for the troubled soul

MEREDITH ARISTONE

Excessive Sodium
a collection of poems for the troubled soul
All Rights Reserved.
Copyright © 2018 Meredith Aristone
v4.0

The opinions expressed in this manuscript are solely the opinions of the author and do not represent the opinions or thoughts of the publisher. The author has represented and warranted full ownership and/or legal right to publish all the materials in this book.

This book may not be reproduced, transmitted, or stored in whole or in part by any means, including graphic, electronic, or mechanical without the express written consent of the publisher except in the case of brief quotations embodied in critical articles and reviews.

Outskirts Press, Inc.
http://www.outskirtspress.com

ISBN: 978-1-4787-9574-2

Cover Photo © 2018 Jeffery Blanford. All rights reserved - used with permission.
Interior Photography © 2018 Jay Rose. All rights reserved - used with permission.
Interior Drawing Water Color © 2018 Oli Boyer. All rights reserved - used with permission.

Outskirts Press and the "OP" logo are trademarks belonging to Outskirts Press, Inc.

PRINTED IN THE UNITED STATES OF AMERICA

Table of Contents

Introduction	1
Ghosts	3
Controlled Chaos	4
Chest Pains	5
Sometimes	6
The Immortality of Plastic	7
Syllables of Wine	9
Lemon Water Diet Coke Love	11
Red	13
Gray	15
What's Up There?	16
The Stages of Connectivity	17
Pain Dance	20
Pain Dance Part II	22
Dandelion Lungs	24
Days	26
Tuesday: I Remember	27
Wednesday: I Feel	28
Thursday: I See	29
Friday: I Regret	30
Chomp	33
Heavy	35
Two Minutes Forty Three Seconds, Medicine	36
Hypochondria	37
Reach Through	39
Time	40
Quilts	41
Numbers	43
Sun vs Moon ☽	**44**

Cigarette Love, Fuck Red Lights	47
Fragments of Truth	48
Perspective	49
Sad Room Full of Ashtrays	50
The Sky	51
What If You're Just Fine?	52
Bored to Tears	53
Understanding My Energies	54
Unfair	55
Hand Talk	56
A Confession	57
A Confession Part 2	58
Cigarette Sun	59
FOMO the end of the beginning	60

INTRODUCTION

IMMODERATE. I was never good at moderation, and I learned that writing was the only healthy outlet for this lack of control that I seem to carry with me in every aspect of my life. One of the most innocent examples of this tendency to exist in excess is my salt addiction, so it quite literally relates to sodium. I put immoderate amounts of salt on everything that I consume, so I thought it would be a comical metaphor for the title.

    I truly realized what an expressive art writing is and learned to embrace the catharsis that lies within carefully crafted brutal honesty. I've come to realize that my growth as a poet and as a person are simultaneous, because each piece that I complete is a conversation with my soul. My art is an extension of my being, so there will always be parallels in my self-discovery and my improvements as a writer. I used to think poetry was about empathy, which in part, it is, because there will always be something rewarding in receiving the emotional sympathies of those who can relate to tragedy and pain, but I've come to realize that it is far more complex than that. My experience with poetry this year taught me that it is about bravery. It is not only an acceptance, but an appreciation of a deep capacity to feel. Poetry doesn't run from emotions - it makes love to them and makes sense of them, no matter how challenging they may be to cope with.

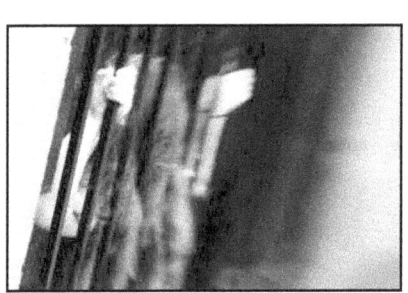

GHOSTS

the purple paint spilled on your neck
looks like venom tonight
when i was the artist,
it was intergalactic watercolor.

I WANT TO FALL THROUGH THE CRACKS IN YOUR VOICE
and open them wider
with my Doc Martens
and stories about July.

i wanna go home
to the warm, chapped valley between your knuckles
to the unappreciated countryside
to our cinematic tug-of-war -
my fangs chewing through the rope of your adoration
to you tying me up with deteriorating wicker

we make a basket and fall asleep.

the rivers in your eyes freeze over before they have a chance to reach
flesh
cold air is unapologetic, angry
and stealing my favorite waterfalls.

you run into the sunset of my hair without fear of being burned
and i scorch you
we are both electrocuted
let's laugh.

CONTROLLED CHAOS

Its 7:17 PM
And I'm donating my body heat to the green couch in the empty house
Relying on the tornado in my skull
To keep me entertained
And the IPA between my fingers is breaking out into a cold sweat

I am grinding my teeth
Hoping that the repressed cries of helplessness
Will disintegrate beneath their fury
Like the snowy powder inside of the rocket ship capsule

Its 7:18 PM
And I am on Mars.

All of my friends are dilated-eyed aliens
And I'm relying on the earthquakes in their hearts
To help me pretend that love is real

CHEST PAINS

Sometimes I fear
That my heart
Is going to make an obstinate escape from my chest

> Imprisoned by its responsibility as a delicate drum kit
> Exhausted by its title as headquarters for passion
> It will
> Flee
> Jump
> Fall
> And make love to the pavement by your shoes.

It demands to be drowned by the bitter words of city air
Restless within the rib cage prison bars
Ticking 60 to 100 times each minute
60 chants turn cries turn screams
60 to 100 chants
Let go

SOMETIMES

Sometimes I miss you softly and
Sometimes I miss you in a way that is more rigid
And sometimes I'm not sure
If I miss you at all

Sometimes the feeling is jagged and penetrative like a knife repeatedly entering and exiting my rib cage
Until my bones are unhinged and collapsing
Like dominos

Sometimes your absence sits in the pit of my stomach in the form of
A dull pain, a mild nauseous darkness loitering until my insides feel as though they are rotting slowly

Sometimes I have to convince myself that I don't taste your name, sour in my mouth
Lingering on the tip of my tongue
Decaying my teeth
In casual conversation

And sometimes I believe that there is a sugary, gooey, liberating relief in being able to dance around your initials in the past tense
These are the days in which I am convinced that the world is still spinning
Even if you are not spinning my world.

THE IMMORTALITY OF PLASTIC

We tie our shoes quickly to forget that the Earth is moving slowly
And that each one of us are only tiny pastel shards of this stained glass universe
That will shatter and be rebuilt on schedule by God or dump trucks or poets

We like to rely on dictionaries, numbers and labels so that we can obtain a sense of certainty
Wrap up in the familiar embrace of systematic exactness, to distract us from the terrifying and inevitable sea of temporary by which we are surrounded
We are in love with permanence because it is instinctive to want what we will never have
Permanence is a controlled substance
Like love
And cocaine

When I combust
I want to bleed
I want to bleed red and blue and stardust and brutally honest venom
I want to watch it drip off of my bones
and taint the human architecture that we all share
With a visual note regarding who I was
And leave a mural of purple on the street
So the body that inherits my soul can make substantive snow angels
And learn about hope
And understand that even though the rain and footsteps of their peers will wash it away
That just because it's temporary
Doesn't mean it was never there

SYLLABLES OF WINE

My name on your red wine tongue
Begins to taste more stale
With every syllable

We're drinking rainwater to avoid
Drowning
To become part of the tsunami
Rather than victims of it

There's cold coffee
In your dilated eyes
And I wonder today
Which artificial sweetener I am

Cappuccino thoughts
Lick the independent melody at the bottom of the mug
fleeting warmth

There are shards of the sunset in my hair
Strawberry fields
But not
Forever

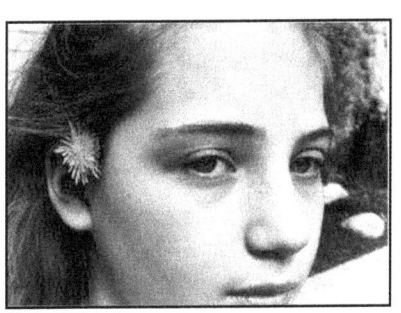

LEMON WATER DIET COKE LOVE

Friday tastes like Monday at the bottom of this bathroom stall, lukewarm pike roast
I'm dizzy
But you taste like hard candy relief
I miss my bed and I miss you in it
I can't find peace
So I find pieces of peace in your passenger seat

I'm still violently rearranging my insides
But you make me feel like there might be some love hiding beneath the rotting flesh

I was always scared of bandaids
And the way they fall off in the shower
There's still blood in our bodies even if it's not oxygenated and staining our skin and clothes and sheets in red
I was scared of forever and what ifs and introducing your lips to my cheek to my heart
But when we talked in angry tongues on that North Philly rooftop, You felt 'mine.'
And my cheeks apologized for the daggers and ice in my soul by permissing you to paint them August-sky-at-sunset pink

And we're lunatics on the Ben Franklin at 2 AM
You let me drive your car as I slip in and out of my vodka adrenaline coma
Like we have something to run away from
And maybe the distorted fireworks in our hearts
Are going to learn how to beat
In sync

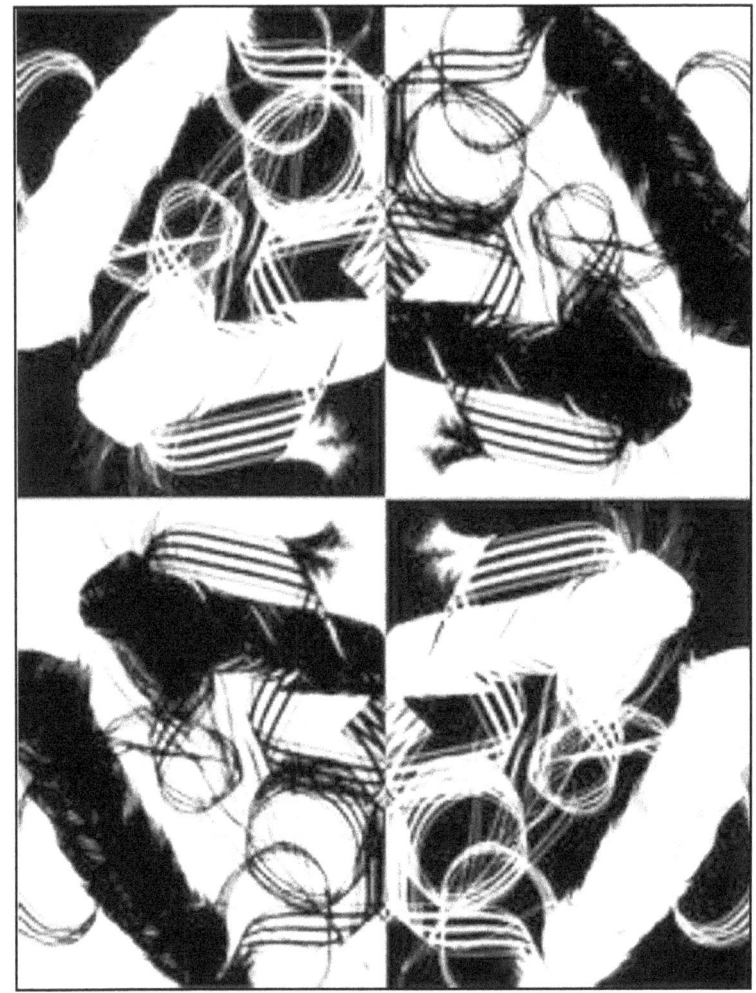

RED

you bite at my soul the way you bite at your fingernails and everyone is nervous the roses are wilting our words are losing meaning you sink your fangs into my neck like you want to create a mural composed entirely of my insides and I'll bleed for you so you have something to paint with you said red's my favorite color for a reason

GRAY

i am swimming against the current in my river of thoughts gasping for air i am breaking glass and the rules and my mess of a mind is scattered on the kitchen floor in bloody shards and his heart is being held hostage by the promise of stability while i am a slave to the chaos i am writing his initials in ballpoint ink on the pages that are falling out of my notebook but cling to their origin of binding with wispy hope and he is smudging my words with a wet violent thumb he is erasing me reducing me to pencil reducing me to gray all he can see is gray

WHAT'S UP THERE?

dear god,
Please
Forgive me for abandoning religion
So recklessly i decided that to save me would be your burden and to become unsalvageable would be my crime
Forgive me for fucking in the parking lot of your house
Leaving my inability to love and my cigarette butts in the cracks of your sidewalk
For leaving my truth on the tongue of someone who is not fluent in your language
Maybe you can teach me how to speak the language of sunlight someday

I am a sinner
If and when
When and if
I stain the white bedsheets pink with the vomit of the tulips I picked from their homes and rubbed across my scalp to experience the essence of change amidst repetitive toxicity
I get some on my fingers and lick it off one by one with my pink sunset tongue
Looking pink like Southern California and flushed cheeks
Feeling blue like Alaska and seeing stars to escape
He left a note with his initials inside of my body
And he wrote in pink ink
But he never said what I would like to
Dear GOD I'm sorry
IF YOU'RE REAL

THE STAGES OF CONNECTIVITY

1. ON FRIENDSHIP: Some people are givers and some are takers. Ravenously, in an attempt to become whole, to glue their shattered pieces together, they will latch onto yours and TAKE. They will take, they will take, and take and take and take. They will tear your organs from your insides and devour them for breakfast without bothering to whisper a thank you for the protein. When your body is ablaze in the heat of life's tumult, encompassed by unforgiving flames, they will watch from a distance and drink every last sip of the water in the hose that they possess because THEY are thirsty. You will tear pills from their clenched fists and dry throat at one AM and flush them down the toilet in a drunken attempt to preserve life, and when they've stopped crying they will call you the next morning to yell at you for wasting the last of their expensive medication. You'll watch the road in determined silence while they drive and prevent them on multiple occasions from vehicular catastrophe. In response, they will call you bossy through a heavy cloud of smoke, it will be blown in your face. you won't cough. You are an ashtray and they are an asshole. Extricate them from your system immediately- the doctors don't recommend toxins.

2. ON LOVE: Some people are soul and some are skin. A true lover should leave hickies that resemble galaxies and not bruises, and a trail of kisses across your body as if you are an unfinished painting and it is up to them to delicately contribute, without ruining the progress that has been made- that you have made. They will look at you as if your eyes are made of sunlight, your bones of charmed amethyst. They care about making you cum first, only you, always you. Your ecstasy is a blossoming flower, vibrant and valid and important to the earth. The pieces of yourself that you offer to them shall become a part of their collection of souls, like vintage, magical books on a library shelf- they are to be cherished and cared for and protected from the pains of the world while in their possession. They will plant roses in your ribs when it is late at night and you say you can't breathe, they'll adore the gap in your teeth and the constellations on your face, they won't mind when you smell like nicotine. They'll bring you coffee on the bad days and daisies on the good ones and let you drive their car down the highway with bare feet on the pedals, no particular destination in mind. You must only welcome those into your body who treat it as if it is a home, not a motel or a pitstop for their pleasure.

3. ON LOSS: It will sneak up on you and scream your name in the language of a blaring alarm on a morning you are far from prepared for. It will drag you out of bed and move your limbs with robotic, relentless force- or it will keep you there forever. And holy fuck, will it sting. It won't just sting, it will burn- burn like hot coffee being splattered all over your favorite T-shirt, seeping through the fabric and scorching your skin with angry determination. It will kiss you with its sharp teeth until your lips are bleeding and you're having trouble resisting the physical urge to set your hollow shell of flesh on fire with a torch. It will reach into your stomach and empty its' contents at 3 in the morning when you thought things were starting to get better. You'll know when it's actually starting to get better because your mouth will taste less like copper and more like flat soda or aged whiskey. You'll be able to watch your favorite Disney movies again and stop avoiding mirrors.

4. ON CONFIDENCE: Confidence is like a yo-yo. It can hit the ground with a heart-shattering thud as quickly as it can ricochet into the ethereal blue abyss of euphoric sky. Play with it, don't play with it too much. If you lose it, buy some more if it at your local dollar store. Touch the small of your back and the curve of your hips because you are an independent film. You are long stretches of road and barefeet and tongue to cheek kisses, hand to hip to breast to ass, you are electric. The world is your forcefield and your veins are filled with bravery and brutality and honesty. Let your loud laugh echo through the thick June air because you can, because it is a melody of liberty, an anthem for your particular genre of soul. Care-fucking-free and that's how you like it. Like it, love it, roll around it as if it is dirt beneath which gold and dead poets have been buried.

PAIN DANCE

When the lonely bares its' teeth, it feels like angry electricity striking a vulnerable wire, snaking itself through each rung of my rib cage, ricocheting off of my bones and scorching the marrow, threatening to become a full body inferno - always loud, and in demand of attention, but consistently refusing to offer a solution. They say it's just a rough patch, but it's not really. There's no such thing as a single rough patch or rough stitch - I am under an entire rough quilt. It is a sad excuse for a blanket that can't seem to assist me in maintaining warmth in a fight against the unforgiving chills of vacancy, the emptiness that throws its hands around my neck and breathes clouds of icy air across my shoulders until my temperature is dipping to dangerous levels and my cheeks are painted purple and blue, shades of twisted galaxies and unretrievable memories.

It announces its presence like a neon sign, flashing behind my eyelids, when the exhaustion is inescapable and sleep is impossible to catch, no matter how far my arms are extended to try and grab it. I am paralyzed with sadness, drowning in it, sinking in a quicksand of hopelessness, unable to ring myself out to dry because I can't find the sunlight, and even the summer isn't powerful enough to promise successful combat of the bitter demons that play tag in my skull and feast on my brain at brunch. They hum their 3 am anthem, smug thieves of the fleeting tranquility I attempted to hold hostage, but dropped in the ash-filled sidewalk cracks through the space between my dried out fingers. They demand that I NEED that I CRAVE that I FEEL

When I spent so long trying to master the art of doing the opposite, doing otherwise, doing anything that didn't require my heart to live in someone else's clenched fists to beat rhythmically - to beat at all.

And they say it won't be like this forever, but their smiles are coated in overpriced cosmetics and deceit, because who's to put an expiration date on something that is already sour? Who is to put a bandaid on a wound that stays open, even when it isn't bleeding? They act as if the damage can be undone, retracted, erased, as though I won't feel like I wasted my chances of being happy laying on the dusty living room couch with open eyes and a closed mind, making enemies with mirrors and friends with broken glass, as if I won't continue to blame myself for the lonely as though my perpetual inability to engage is not a character flaw I despise?

They act as though I won't remember this if I get a chance to kiss the sky's baby pink hues again, if they are warm and fresh on my tongue

PAIN DANCE PART II

   maybe I will lose all of the hateful words in the back of my throat and instead sing with the birds, romantic and poetic and passionate I am nothing if not passionate Good fucking morning I will remember to thank all of the lucky stars and the unlucky ones too, that I am still alive, that I didn't slip away into the grasp of the sad as I tossed and turned in the gray space prison, shouted into the void, the neverending abyss and wrestled with the urge to not nurture the backwards math and the frontwards witchcraft, the dysmorphia, haunting, repetitive and cyclical, like a nursery rhyme see

   i am a wet rose with all of the thorns out, and I am the most expensive china littering the wood floor, shattered in every place, ready to cut the calloused ankles of the uncareful and inconsiderate walkers don't you dare tiptoe through my void without paying the toll that I have paid to this warped universe and I still scream

   a victim of injustice playing the victim card

   I make all of the noise that I know how to
   until my vocal cords are stretched beyond plausible elasticity and demand the answers to questions that no one has the audacity to ask

   heaven probably isn't even white its' red with the blood of the lovers that died in the fight and dirtied the clouds with their heavy explosive hearts

   I mean GOD i'm so fucking sick of having reason on top of reason to beg the pain to take a hiatus
   to beg the sky to rain novacaine

gel me up with the numbing paint and flatten me into the canvas so I can watch the dimensional delusional human beings fight with authenticity and swallow full teaspoons of sugar to satiate their sweet tooth when the loving isn't good when the loving isn't in season

and OH GOD I demanded truth I wanted to feel it in my bones but I wanted to share the taste of it with lips that were not made of styrofoam that is just a metaphor I do not feel beautiful anymore I cannot fucking bear to do this alone to watch everything crumble and be broken to watch all of the parts of the things that used to run sit in a pile and RUST and fuck i know they say be careful what you wish for but I was always a time bomb

DANDELION LUNGS

There is a garden in my lungs
But all I can taste is
Dirt
No, that's not true
Almost true
Not completely
I can taste the ink bleeding through the pages, a result of my exhausted, messy penmanship
And his sandpaper knuckles, raw with confusion
The way I form my E's just like my grandfather
Strawberries in the mornings
Thick August air
Slow August morning
Dry mouth, cotton mouth
My cotton-mouthed mourning
And dirt
I picture the petals of the dying flowers in my ribcage
Curling themselves around each rung
Leaving their last drops of nectar and vibrancy to me
As a solemn gift
Generous pink daisies
Selfless daisies, selfish daisies?
Pastel reminders
Of my selfishness
I am determined to be alone with the sunset
I swallow it
It, too, is pink
But I taste golden goodbyes
Hazardous horizons

There are seeds in his mouth
I am greedy
I suck them out with my tongue
Tongue to cheek poetry
Tongue to cheek to hip to breast
Tongue to cheek poetry demands growth
Grow, grow, grow
I scream at my garden to grow
I inhale
Grow, please grow
And all I see is
Dirt

DAYS

monday: i want
i want you out of my mind and under my sheets
you want me out of your mind and under the ground
we trip and fall out of love
instead we fall asleep

tuesday: i remember

    i remember my name for you and your names for me and our names for the strange tornado of electricity in our stomachs when we kissed

    i remember the first time and the last time and the intoxicating urge to retrieve the ashes of the love that i cremated

    i remember the slammed doors falling off of their hinges the open doors the violent curious temptation to escape the trap of numbness to tear off the bandaid and the neosporin to reopen the wound and never let it heal

wednesday: i feel

    i feel you in my veins in my basement in my stomach your hands are in my hair your thumb is grazing my heart and there is something tender in your eyes that creates the illusion of permanence

    you appear in a cloud of marijuana induced blurriness and i'm not sure if its a dream or a nightmare but i feel you with me even when you are not mine to touch

thursday: i see

    sometimes i see you through half closed lids in the bottom of my dented red solo cup and i see you screaming at me through the cracks in the ground you are a red wine stain on the carpet you are the sky you are heaven there are some days when i am sure that i will see you when i die in a vision in a blur of light *you are my delusions and my certainties* you are my bruises *you are all of my bruises* and i watch you taint my skin with your discolored art

friday: i regret

it turns out i didn't learn how to run in high school cross country practices, i learned how to run when your lips touched my forehead and you saw my demons escape my chest in heavy sobs and held my hand all the way through you were sugar and i was salt desperately searching for some wounds to burn i regret my jagged escape from the comfort of your arms

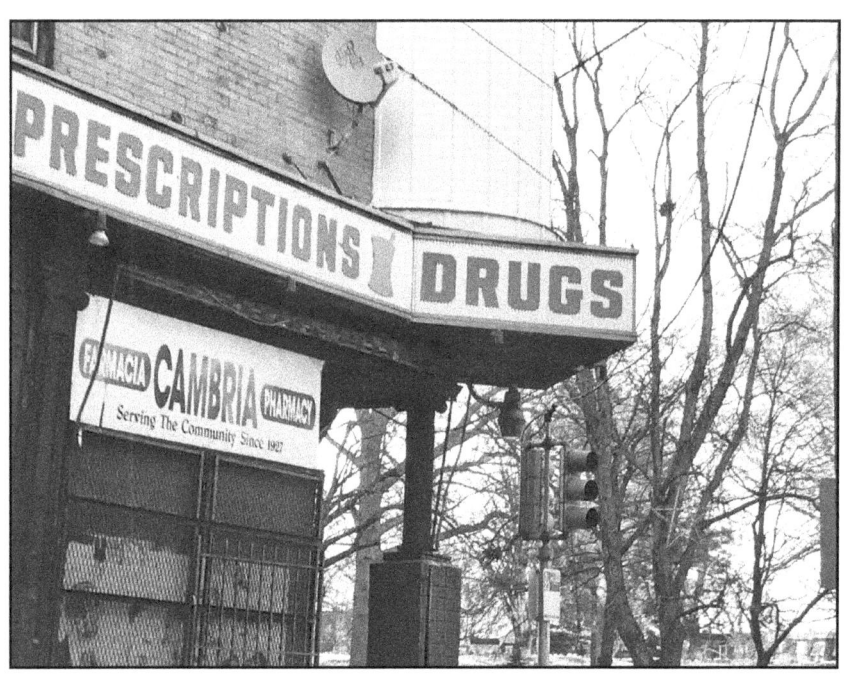

CHOMP

i want to suck my soul dry of you to chew the remains of the whispered words you left out of my mouth to crush them beneath gritted teeth until i am all out of material all out of lowercase and uppercase goodbyes until i am sick of trying to remember tired of trying to forget until there is nothing in my mind that is tainted by your name until i can see the sky as blue and not the color of your eyes until i can start over until there is poetry in the veins of someone else's arms and balance in the way they hold me i want to pump you out of my stomach and beat you out of my heart

HEAVY

Why do I always need to be as empty as I feel?
A perverse attempt at balance
I starve my body and nourish my demons
And somehow (paradoxically enough) I am still heavy
With my thoughts and the way they settle in my stomach like bricks
With the weight of the tears I won't release until I can cry rose petals or liquid gold
With the hope that one day you'll understand
I don't want empathy
I want comprehension

Gut-wrenching, finger shaking, arm numbing, fists through the wall in sync comprehension
And maybe I'm selfish for that
But it's tiring, lugging this dirty laundry bag of hostility and sadness and confusion on the back of my 5'3 frame alone

It's heavy

TWO MINUTES FORTY THREE SECONDS , MEDICINE

2:43 seconds remaining on my alarm, 2:43 seconds till sunlight, till death, till pretending to listen. your eyes are glowing but your words are meaningless, echoing through my hollow skull - i swallow them like they're medicine, but even if you're speaking fluent aspirin, i need to sleep before the headache retreats. i wake up and apologize for my illness. you tell me that you're not afraid to catch it. your eyes are hot coffee with cubes of sugar and i am diving into them, making them lukewarm with the ice in my blood, swallowing up the sweetness and replacing it with something artificial, like splenda, and pinky promises with my fingers crossed behind my back. we know bathroom floors and slurred words and slurred words on bathroom floors like a second language. i think you're in love with the idea of me, you think you're in love with my freckles. you want to be honey on my sore throat, but i have become so good at spitting out every drop of gooey relief you offer me, at embracing and spreading the burn.

something inside of me wants to be yours. something inside of me is angry and restless and unresolved. I was cut in half before i was finished growing. i am always searching. something inside of me is quaking.

and sometimes you touch something soft within me with your smile and your foot so readily on the gas pedal of your car, always willing to propel us away from reality and into someone else's sunset. sometimes your body is more than a skeleton, you become enough to keep me warm. sometimes i fall in love with your spontaneous and your eyelashes on my cheek and the way kisses taste wrapped in coffee and rum and letting go. sometimes i want to walk on tightropes with you, and sometimes i wish you would just push me off.

HYPOCHONDRIA

it's not real unless it hurts
and if it hurts, it's my reality
so the anxiety bares its' teeth and peels my eyes open, forcing me to exist in a state of conscious agitation for the ugliest parts of 2 am
and they're banging on the door
afraid of what i've created afraid of what the world has weathered me into
always convinced that i am already on my way to being a ghost

my arms are numb and my mouth tastes like dish soap and i am convinced that the doctors are lying
baffled when i wake up to regular breathing
angry at the IV when it is an intruder in my arm and terrified by the possible impurities in my blood when it is removed
wearing the hospital bracelet like a badge like a nametag like the only thing that is honest
yes i'm a mess and i need to prove that my thoughts are catastrophically waging a war on my body
i need to prove that it's real
that this ugly disease makes me a little bit less than alive

and i mean, you know

there's a twisted part of me that expects bad news so i insist
 on convincing myself that my blood is black and infected by poison
so i can see the hot glow of red lights behind my eyelids
when i need to slam on the breaks and life won't let me

it's the irony, too
the terrifying paradox that a hospital could be a safehouse a lifeboat
that this is where people come to die and it's where i come to wonder
if i'm too tired to keep living
i take life so fucking for granted and then i feel guilty that i'm not appreciating things like sunlight in my window and food on my tongue
so i punish myself subconsciously
and suddenly everything just HURTS

and it's really a game of russian roulette i think
i push and i push and i push and as long as i'm winning when the moncy's spent and the tests are over i keep pushing

REACH THROUGH

we start the night as amphetamine fueled ghosts
lingering between our pasts and our present in a dimly lit hallway
gazing through doorways but never opening doors
contorting our features into a variety of expressions just to make
sure the muscles still work
moving in place because there's nowhere to run to
yet somehow we're all running anyway with every exhaled word
cheap beer and insincerities dripping off of our tongues
i think i could reach through everyone in this room

TIME

time doesn't exist, but somehow it still limits us
it is a construct and so are we
so we build an existence of illusionary guidance
to help us feel bigger
than what we are

QUILTS

i have no control
i am out of control out of my mind out of answers
out of coping mechanisms

i dropped some of them out of the window on the drunk car ride here
and lost the rest in between the couch cushions where i fell in lust for the third? time

and their voices are like sandpaper
they do a tango of misery in the kitchen
sometimes i laugh sometimes i shut my eyes sometimes i throw up
some days i feel like the piece of jenga that was removed from the tower to make everything collapse
some days i feel like the tower is crumbling on top of me
some days i wish i remembered what it's like to look at a flower and not imagine tearing it to shreds petal by petal because one day it's going to wilt anyway and true finiteness is either temporary or an illusion right

i don't know if there's a such thing as unbroken families or happy people or if we're all just jagged puzzle pieces floating around this earth hanging on with glue and bandaids and false hope
i don't know if there's a such thing as love or if we cannot bear to be freeze so we attach our skeletal selves to the closest source of body heat within a 5 mile radius

i don't know if i'm ever going to get better

what defines getting better, anyway?
i mean what does that narrative look like?
do i pass a mirror and suddenly see an untouched porcelain doll instead of the cynical raggedy anne that i've become
do i forget that i am made of cracked ice and wildfires and 3 am and stale liquor breath
all of my words coated in nicotine and skepticism
do i pretend that all i know is the sweet, romantic embrace of 6 am sunlight and orange juice and daisies
do i pretend that i've never been shattered that i've never felt a hole

because maybe we're meant to feel internal holes
maybe the breeze needs to get into our souls occasionally
maybe we need to know how to hate and ache the same way that we try to learn how to love and fight
maybe that's a justified part of life
everyone spends so much time trying to patch their holes and disguise their voids
we're all walking around like fucking quilts

maybe we should let our wounds breathe
so we can finally breathe, too.

NUMBERS

1. sometimes it's not that people don't care, it's that they *can't* care
2. i don't think that you wanting to be happy was selfish
3. starting over is never selfish
4. starting over is brave and how could i blame you?
5. In some way or another, i hope to start over every day

SUN VS MOON ☽

The moon isn't mad at me, but the sun is.

CIGARETTE LOVE, FUCK RED LIGHTS

we're driving through this half-hearted cigarette love
and i think about the things i can control and the things that i can't
with one hand on the steering wheel, the other on his heart
i can control how fast this vehicle moves
whether it spirals out of control in a flurry of passion beneath the
judgmental glare of red lights
or collides with another lost soul

FRAGMENTS OF TRUTH

Sometimes i feel like i'm fragments of truth and fragments of a lie and only fragments of myself
We might all be crawling around this earth, confused skeletons and puzzle pieces

PERSPECTIVE

How can we be whole if we are all fragments of eachother?
How can we know what we're searching for if we've always been lost?
And now I'm lying on the carpet of a hotel corridor
Hearing sounds, but not listening to them
I stopped listening tonight, I stopped listening a while ago
I am seeing things but I am not watching them
I am understanding things but I am not appreciating them
Or maybe I'm entirely wrong..
Maybe to understand is to appreciate
Maybe the concrete and the abstract are holding hands and laughing at us
Maybe the rain is the sun's tears of joy
Maybe God is a scientist and Manhattan is a small town
And loneliness is merely a friendship with our demons

SAD ROOM FULL OF ASHTRAYS

This room is sad
It's not mine, but it's crying out to me
Breathing its' cold musty air into my face

This room is dark
It's not mine, but it is reaching into my body
Feeling for pieces of tangibility that could fill its' empty

This room is begging someone to love

This room is begging someone to stay

THE SKY

The sky is half golden and half white as if it can't make up its mind
So I guess we have that in common

WHAT IF YOU'RE JUST FINE?

A simple question
To which I always presume the answer is no

I insist that I don't know how to be
And she proposes the notion that even if I don't know how to be, I am

What if I'm just fine?

Then, what?

BORED TO TEARS

I think I left my ability to 'just be' somewhere in the gravel of the Pocono Mountains or between North Philly's sidewalk cracks because tonight, each of my sober breaths are heavy in my chest with the weight of restlessness, short with impatience and like my dreams, hard to catch.

If I'm not speaking the language of love letters, if any of my words aren't released in a cloud of fiery determination, then I am suddenly no longer a dragon. I miss my wings.

I cannot stand being caught in the rain because being caught sounds like being trapped and being trapped sounds like having nowhere to go and having nowhere to go sounds like having nowhere to be and having nowhere to be makes me feel like I have no one to love and having no one to love makes me feel small. small. It makes me think about the space that I occupy. Which isn't a lot. small. And thinking about space makes me think about time. Wasted time makes me wish I were wasted. So I could waste even more of it.

I hate to be morbid, but I think I hate dishonesty more. Lying by omission is dishonesty and our chronic refusal to acknowledge our slowly (but constantly) decaying human condition is just that. I would rather spend all of the time before I die being alive. You say that I am but I promise you, I'm not.

I think I first experienced being truly alive in a dream, then on a rollercoaster, then on an airplane, then in a person's arms. Not here.

Restless souls weren't meant for resting.

Another year.

I finally know what they meant when they said bored to tears.

UNDERSTANDING MY ENERGIES

I can't tell if this energy is nervous energy or creative energy, fear of being alone or desperate craving for my space. I'm trying to make sense of myself, and this world, and myself in this world. I am navigating the tunnel of irrational fear and the loneliness that hides inside of it, on my journey towards the mountains of truth drizzled in sunlight that I can only hope will receive my less troubled soul with open arms when I reach the other side. I am finally grabbing for my dreams in their tightly sealed envelope under my bed, thinking about how I've kept them hidden for so long in the same place I was convinced monsters resided as a child. I've spent so much of my time on mindlessness in hopes of wrapping my arms around distraction and having it return the hug with the numbing sensation that is the comfort of oblivion, but I am ready to abandon that crutch. I am ready to grow new legs and walk on my own, to climb out of the hollow shell of the person I was. I was made of excuses and addictions, I cried tears of rubbing alcohol and carelessly spilled salt in my own wounds. I fought time and it's burdensome inevitability. No, not fought, waged WAR on time, despite the fact that I knew it would always win. Today I am made of fire and acceptance. I hope to understand. I choose to love. I will always carry mistakes with me, because no one travels without baggage, but I refuse to be tainted by them. Instead, I am glowing with the lessons I have learned and the tears I've sewn back together. Some things look better patched up, anyway.
I am learning to blame myself less and love myself more, to understand that my limbs aren't tools for destruction but pieces of art, that my thoughts will be out of my control from time to time, but the universe has a plan. I am understanding my energies.

UNFAIR

you are the type of lover to punch me in the face and complain that your fists hurt but I love you so much that I would call the bruises galaxies

HAND TALK

why do people talk with their hands?
it is as if our voices aren't enough
sound vibrations could never be enough to imitate what our hollow
bodies are feeling
what we want to feel
the art of explaining

A CONFESSION

Addiction isn't the thing that I'm addicted to, it's the thing that I'm missing.

A CONFESSION PART 2

You can be alone, but you don't want to.
I can't be alone, but I wish I was.

CIGARETTE SUN

I love the way a lit cigarette looks in my mouth, like I could swallow the sun if it didn't burn my lips first, so that my unspoken words are forever imprisoned in an ashy chamber. There's so much and so little to life in the slowly disintegrating space between my index and forefingers.

FOMO
the end of the beginning

    This feeling was born somewhere deep in my stomach and set up home there, refusing to migrate, even when the winter came. Especially when the winter came. I feel like I'm always waiting. For trains, answers, dreams, the right lover, the wrong one. My entire life has been spent teetering on the unforgiving tightrope of desire between my heart and my soul and I'm scared of falling but at the same time I want nothing more than to plunge, to be pushed to be shoved, but more than that, I want to not NEED to be pushed or shoved. I want to have the courage to jump.

    I'm not necessarily talking about death, when I say plunge. I mean I want to find something permanent in the adrenaline I always chase. Is there such thing as a permanent feeling if human emotions are like the ocean? Because there's certainly not a such thing as a permanent wave.

    Words are beautiful and so are flowers. But flowers don't really mean anything to us (most of the time) unless they're being plucked from their homes in the ground and delivered to the hands of a human soul out of love or loss or apology. So I want to pluck these words from their home in my head and deliver them to your mind. I want to leave this book in the world as a genuine piece of my humanity. This is as permanent as I know how to be. This is Excessive Sodium.

Lightning Source UK Ltd.
Milton Keynes UK
UKHW011322160120
357073UK00001B/94/P